The Girl with the Healing Hands

Csongor Daniel

To Kylie and Karlyn with love.

Printed in the United States of America
Library of Congress Control Number: 2008900790
ISBN: 0-9658781-4-7
Illustrations: Kylie Daniel and Csongor Daniel
Page design: Csongor Daniel
Cover design: Anna Krecicki, Kylie Daniel and Csongor Daniel

2733 Lawyer Terrace
North Port, FL 34288
(941) 423-7901
www.csongordaniel.com

PROLOGUE

I had been practicing energy medicine for ten years when my first daughter, Kylie, was born. Since my healing abilities developed only in my early twenties, I was looking forward to teaching Kylie all about this special gift at a much earlier age. I didn't have to put in much effort. She had a born talent for healing. At the age of two, she could already stop other people's pain. Developing such a special power would take a lot of work and concentration for an adult. But for a child, it is just a game. Kylie loved the game. This book is written to all the children who would like to learn to heal.

The Baby

Kylie's hands can heal. That's right; the hands of a five year old can take away pain! How can that be? You'll find out through her story.

Kylie was a young girl like any other: special. Yes, everybody is special. We each have our own individual personalities, and that makes each of us unique. But there was something about her that even she didn't know. She was going to find out that she had magical powers. By the end of the story you will find out that you have these powers, too!

It all started before Kylie was born, when she was in her Mommy's belly - a comfortable, warm, and cozy place where there were no worries at all. She shared everything with her Mommy: food, drinks, even music that seemed to have filled her whole body. Sometimes it was light, sometimes it was dark, but it was always pleasant and safe. Often, there was another feeling, one hard to describe. A tingly warmth that came from the outside. Usually, it was accompanied by a deeper sound. Was it someone's voice? Was it nature? Was it real or just her imagination? How could she know? She wasn't even born yet.

After her dazzling birth, Kylie's life was very exciting. Like all babies, she loved exploring her new surroundings. There was so much to experience in this new world! So many colors, shades, shapes, smells and tastes! Who could name them all? Best of all, the warmth she had experienced in her Mommy's belly before her birth, was still there. Every time Mommy picked her up, she had the same sensation of safety and comfort. There was also another comfy person. He was as tingly and warm as she remembered. The person with the deep voice. It was her Daddy.

At the beginning Daddy was just a simple daddy. He didn't do much. He just cuddled her a lot and watched Mommy do everything else. Mommy was very good at feeding, bathing, dressing, and taking care of her little baby. She even got up several times every night just to please Kylie's growling little stomach.

It took Daddy a while before he caught up. He slowly learned how to change diapers, how to dress Kylie, how to feed her, and how to do so many other things that he had never done before. It was so funny to see him struggle with the dirty diapers, trying hard not to dirty himself! Folding them the way Mommy taught him was hard at first. Kylie knew that Daddy would never be as good at those things as Mommy, but then, something happened that made her realize that he had other gifts to share with her.

Babies drink so much sweet, tasty milk that it sometimes makes their stomachs hurt. One day when that happened to Kylie, Daddy came to the rescue. He picked her up gently. All of a sudden the pain started fading away! His hand on her back felt warmer and warmer, soothing her whole body. That familiar tingly feeling was there, too. Then there was no pain at all!

Kylie was too young to talk, but she was not too young to know that somehow her Daddy could make pain stop with this warm and tingly feeling. She knew she wanted Daddy around whenever something hurt. If Kylie could not fall asleep, Daddy would wave his hands over her, without even touching her. Her eyes would get heavy, and her whole body would sink gently into a soft baby dream world.

The Healer

Daddy knew exactly what Kylie needed when she hurt or couldn't sleep. He knew about the special forces that can be used to stop pain or just to make someone feel good. Daddy was a healer.

Healers are special individuals who know how to make other people stop hurting and help sick people feel better.

When Daddy was a little boy, he found out that he had this special gift. As he was growing up he realized that everybody has a similar gift. Just like everybody can learn to read and write, or ride a bicycle, or even play the piano, we can all learn to heal ourselves and others. And even though some of us are better at reading, or writing, or biking, and some at playing the piano, we can all learn to do all of those things. We can do anything as long as we really want to. We can even learn to heal.

Kylie was too young to know that Daddy was teaching her things. He wanted his daughter to be healthy and happy, so he decided to teach her everything about healing from a very early age. He started even before she was born. The tingly warm feeling coming from the outside, while Kylie was in her Mommy's belly, was indeed her Daddy's healing energy.

Kylie always knew when he was doing his magic. It felt so good! Soon she was able to tell the difference between when Daddy was just "regular dad," and when he was actually using his healing power.

After a while, she realized that she could not just feel, but even see the difference. Sometimes there would be a fog around Daddy's hands. Sometimes she could see it around his whole body. As she grew older, Kylie was able to see this foggy, misty, and smoky "something" around everyone, even around animals and plants. As she later learned, this "something" is called an aura.

The most fun she had was when Daddy showed her how they could be connected without touching each other. Daddy would start by turning the palms of his hands toward Kylie. She would see the energy right away. She would then raise her hands, palm out to him. As they reached out with their hands toward one another, she could not only see but even feel the energy connecting them!

Kylie liked to watch Daddy circle his hands a few feet away from her body. She would reach out and follow Daddy's hands. They would not touch, but it felt like they did. They would see a fog between their hands that was always warm and comforting. Soon they began to play this game every day. They would try to see how far apart they could get their hands and still feel each other's energy. They wanted to find ways to see the energy more easily. They experimented to see which part of their hands and bodies would feel the energy the most. The game was a lot of fun. The more they played, the easier it was for Kylie to feel the energy.

The Hands

As Kylie grew bigger and started talking, Daddy was able to explain to her what these things she could feel and see actually were.

One day, Daddy decided to teach her how she could do some energy exercises by herself.

"Hold up your hands in front of your chest. Let your elbows hang, and relax your shoulders," he said. "Keep your hands apart, loosen your fingers and imagine that you are holding a very light ball. Close your eyes and try to see your imaginary ball. Feel how smooth and round it is. Count to ten and start playing with it: Squeeze it a little bit, and then release it back. Do this a few times using very small, fast movements. Can you feel the resistance? It is just like playing with magnets. Have you ever played with magnets? This pushing that you feel is not just because you have a good imagination, but because you have found the edges of one of the layers of your aura, which is your energy field." Daddy then explained to Kylie that this aura surrounds the human body, animals, plants and every object around us. It consists of tiny particles of energy that form an egg-shape field around our bodies. She was amazed!

"Now, let's try it again, but this time, bring your hands closer together, Daddy went on. "It is a very interesting feeling if you do it slowly, inch by inch, and let your hands go back a little bit more each time. Can you feel it push more as your hands get closer together? Now, let's try the opposite way. As you pull your hands away, can you feel them pulling back to the center? Congratulations, Kylie! You can feel your aura! You might even feel some heat or tingling in your hands as you practice. Don't be discouraged if you can't feel it right away. The more you practice, the more you will feel it!"

Kylie was amazed by this new knowledge. She thought it was fun. It wasn't difficult. Within a few days she felt that she was ready to ask Daddy to show her some new exercises. He was happy to help, and eagerly showed her how to do something new.

"Let's start by repeating the first exercise," he said. "Once you can feel the "ball" again, bring your hands closer. Keep your hands flat and your fingers straight, while putting them very close to each other. Start circling them around the middle of your palms. You will feel the energy whirling around the centers of your palms. It usually feels quite warm and tingly."

Kylie tried it. She was able to feel the energy right away!

Daddy said, "Let's go a step further. We will keep one hand open, but only use the pointer finger of the other. Make small circles with your pointer around the middle of your palm. Make sure you don't let them touch. If you can still feel the energy, make bigger circles farther away. See how far you can go without losing the feel of the energy."

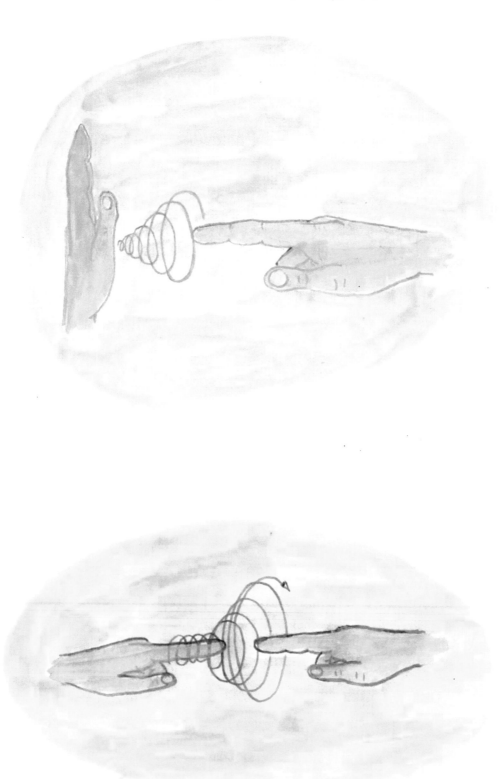

These exercises were a lot of fun, but they didn't stop Kylie from being a regular little girl.

Her Mommy took her to daycare every morning before work. There, she had a lot of little friends to play with. They also took regular naps in the afternoon, so when Mommy picked her up, she was alert and ready for more fun with her family.

In the evenings Kylie, Mommy, and Daddy would go for long walks, play with their dogs, or just sit down and read stories.

After dinner Kylie would get a bath with lots of bubbles and plenty of floating toys. That was her favorite time. Later, in her fresh pajamas, she would brush her teeth, kiss Mommy and Daddy goodnight, and go to bed. But she wouldn't fall asleep right away.

By the light of her night lamp she would play with her energy field. She discovered that she could do the last exercise that Daddy taught her, by using only her two pointers circling them around each other.

One night as Daddy was walking past Kylie's door, he peaked in to check on her. To his amazement, she was playing this very game! He was so happy to see his little girl practicing the energy exercises, that he wanted to teach her as much as he could, as soon as possible. Right away he showed her how to move her hand up and down her arm, and feel the heat in her arm and hand even without touching!

Watching Kylie do this exercise made Daddy very proud. "This is the first serious step toward becoming a healer," he thought. "Maybe she will turn out to be one some day."

The Aura

Kylie had many experiences with seeing the aura - the haziness she noticed around people, plants and animals. However, there were also times when she couldn't see it. She didn't know why.

Her Daddy understood because he used to have the same difficulties when he was young. He had to learn to see the energy the hard way - on his own. "Why not help Kylie skip the difficult part?" he thought.

Daddy knew that more games would help her see the aura, this beautiful display of nature, even more often.

"Let's play a game with our hands," Daddy said. "It will help you to see your own aura better.

"With your arms straight, hold your hands at eye level. Your palms should be facing you. Stretch out your fingers and spread them a little bit apart. Now comes the hard part. Look directly at the area between the fingertips of your middle fingers. Try not to stare at your fingers or at the background. Keep your eyes on the area between your fingertips! Watch it carefully. Can you see something between them? It looks a little bit foggy, doesn't it?"

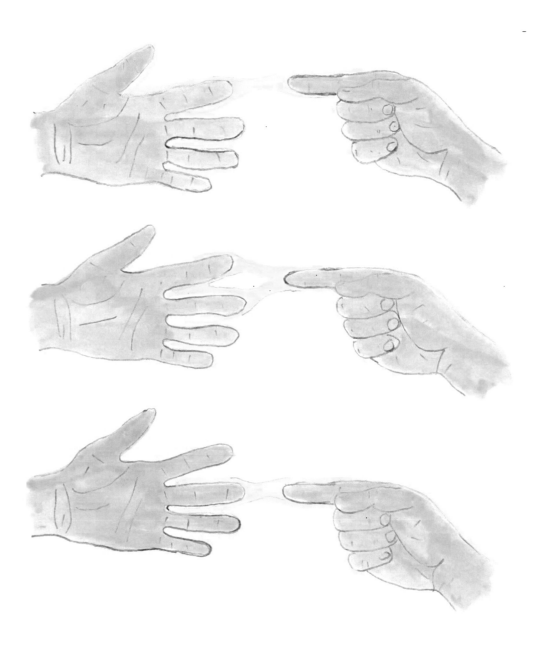

Yes, Kylie could see it. It looked just like that fog she used to see around Daddy's hands and his body before she even knew what it was called.

"You can call it hazy, misty, smoggy, cloudy, or blurry," Daddy said. "It is all around your fingers and even around your whole body. What you see is the first layer of your aura. There are seven layers, but it is not important to see them all."

"If you look very carefully at the fingertip of only one finger, you'll be able to see a little funnel-like light beam coming out of it. Funny, isn't it?

"Now, move your pointer finger up and down along the fingers of your other hand. Don't touch, though! Can you see how the blurry beam from your pointer connects with each of the fingertips on your hand? When your pointer is between two fingers of the other hand, it connects to them both. Try to see how far away you can move your fingers before you lose the beams."

Daddy wanted to make sure that even though Kylie was practicing hard, she was still having fun. She was just a little girl, and this was just a game. Daddy wanted Kylie to enjoy learning to see her aura.

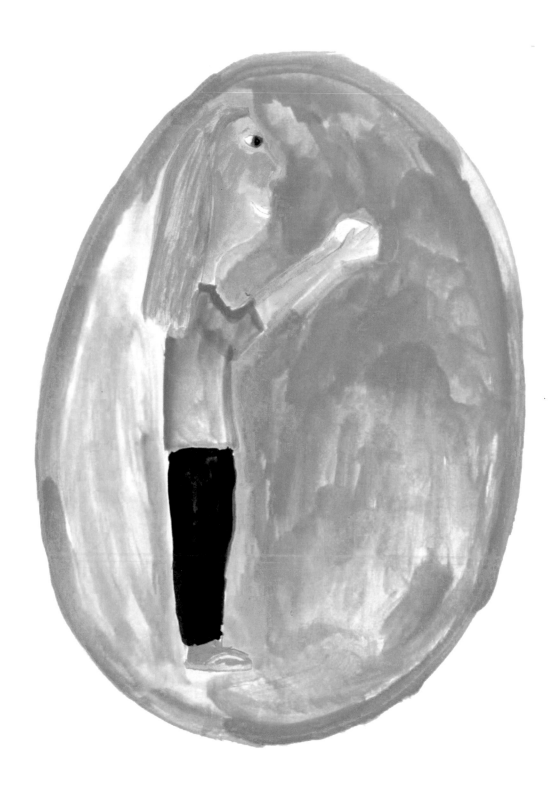

The Teasing

Kylie was an eager learner. She would practice as often as possible, although, sometimes at the wrong time and at the wrong place.

Seeing and feeling the aura is not a common thing. It is very unusual, and thus strange to some people, including other kids. Kylie didn't know that. How could she? She had lived with it her whole life. It was normal for her to see and to feel beyond the "regular" senses. Daddy didn't tell her that and it lead to some confusion in her young life.

One boring rainy day at the daycare Kylie decided to practice, since she had nothing better to do. Little did she know that none of the other kids had ever seen or felt the aura before. Nor did her teacher, Miss Ana.

At first, they all looked at her strangely, then, some of the kids started teasing her. Since they didn't know what she was doing, to them it looked as if she were just playing with the empty air. They were pointing at her and laughing out loud. Even Miss Ana could not stop them.

Kylie was very surprised and hurt. She tried to explain about the energy she was playing with, but none of the kids would listen. They just kept teasing her all day.

When her Mommy picked her up that afternoon, Kylie was in tears. She could not wait to get home and tell her Daddy what happened. Fortunately, he understood right away.

"Well," he said, "I was afraid that would happen one day. I just hoped it would be much later. You see, people are afraid of the unknown. If they can't explain or understand something, they may be scared of it. Some people will try to cover up their fear by being mean, some will just be quiet. Then again, some may just try to be funny. This is true for your little friends, too. It was easier for them to tease you than to understand what you were doing. Don't worry about it. It will pass."

Daddy hoped Kylie would get over this incident as fast as possible. He thought that if she built up more confidence in the energy games, people's reactions wouldn't bother her again. But how was he supposed to help her? How could he build up a little girl's confidence if she was so hurt? The answer came just a day later.

Grandpa

As if called to the rescue, Kylie's grandfather came to visit. He was a big and strong man with a great matching laugh and thick glasses. He was so strong that one time he lifted up the end of a car and held it while his friend changed a flat tire! But, as he got older, his knees hurt. Some days he could hardly walk.

Every time he visited, Daddy would work on his knees to make them feel better. Daddy would gently cup his hands over Grandpa's knees. He would hold his hands there until they got very warm. Then he would sweep his hands away and shake them off. Daddy said this would sweep away Grandpa's pain.

Kylie thought that looked like fun, and she decided to give it a try. For a short moment, she thought of the previous day's teasing. She even thought that maybe it may not work. But in the end, she just wanted to help Daddy fix Grandpa's knees. She began to do everything Daddy did. Kylie held her hands on Grandpa's knees till they got very warm. Then, she slowly pulled out the "bad" energy and shook her hands off.

At first, Grandpa laughed. It was funny to see Kylie imitate her Daddy. But then he turned serious. He began to feel her

energy! There was something going on! Suddenly, the pain faded away. "Wow," said Grandpa turning to Daddy, "there are more of you around here!" His laughter thundered through the house.

Kylie was so thrilled with her success that she instantly forgot about all the teasing from the day before. She was so proud of her magical powers that nothing could wipe the smile off her face.

That was when Daddy decided to teach her some more. He said, "Let's look at Grandpa's energy field." Grandpa was already sitting against the wall, so Daddy said, "Just look at the area over Grandpa's head. Don't look at his head or at the wall. Just look at the area over his head. Can you see the same haziness as you have seen around your hands and fingers? Can you see the misty funnel over his head? That is Grandpa's aura. It is around his whole body. We all have it just like he does!"

Grandpa's knees felt so much better! Daddy decided to ask him a favor. Kylie was still in the mood for more energy-games, and Grandpa could help her play. Daddy asked Grandpa to stand against the wall. Then, Kylie and Daddy would be able to see Grandpa's whole energy field. Daddy explained that it was always better when the lights were a bit dimmed, and there were no other distractions. As Grandpa stood against the wall, Kylie and Daddy concentrated on watching his energy field. They did not look at Grandpa's head or at the wall. They just looked over his head. Kylie could indeed tell where Grandpa's aura ended. She could see it just over his head and around his whole body. Then

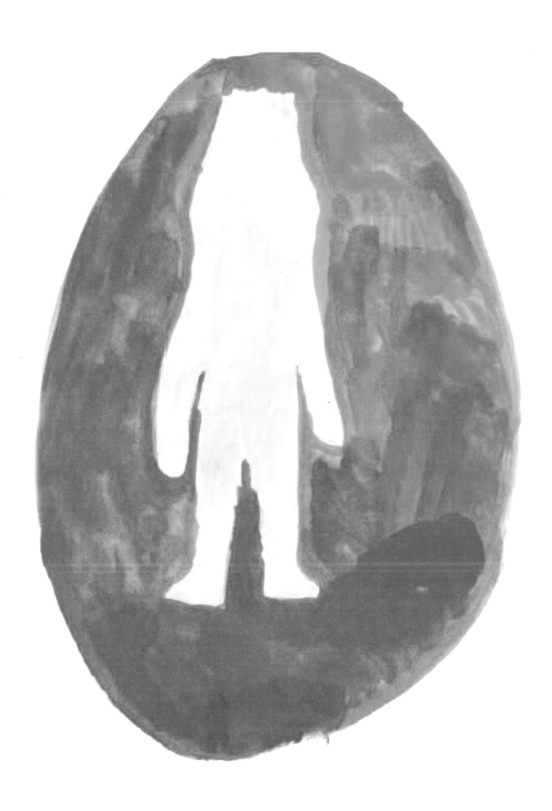

Daddy asked Grandpa to step away from the wall. He told Kylie to keep watching the spot where Grandpa had been standing. It was amazing! As Grandpa walked away from the wall, his aura was still there! It took some time before it faded away.

Afterward, Daddy turned to Kylie and said: "You see, every time you touch something, you leave an energy mark on it. That is because everything is made up of energy. Sometimes, you can even use this to find your way in the darkness. Just feel your way."

Kylie liked that lesson. She didn't feel afraid in the dark anymore. She would just concentrate on feeling the energy around her. It made her feel safe.

The Lecture

"Now, I want to show you that you can actually change your energy field just by changing your thoughts," Daddy said one day. "That is called concentration. I will stand against the wall. Try to see my energy field." Of course, it wasn't hard this time. Daddy's energy field was clear and normal. Then he said, "Now watch the top of my head. I will make my aura grow."

Kylie was amazed! Daddy's aura started growing almost instantly. It went all the way up to the ceiling! Then, he stepped away. The aura was still there!

"That is what I have been trying to teach you. You can do anything as long as you really want it to happen. I wanted to grow my aura and it happened," Daddy said. "It shows you that your mind can change your energy field any time. Sometimes you don't even mean to. Just look at other people's auras when they are in different moods. Their energy fields are much thicker when they are happy and relaxed. When they are sad, the fields are thin and weak. That can make you sick. It is important to concentrate on keeping your aura thick and happy. This will help to keep you healthy." Then he added: "Don't forget that since everything is made of energy, your thoughts apply to everything else in your life.

x

"You can get anything you want, or become anything you want, as long as you want it really hard. Make sure though, to keep those thoughts positive."

"Everything is energy?" wondered Kylie aloud. "Even my Teddy Bear?"

"Yes Kylie," her Daddy answered with a smile, "even your Teddy Bear.

"Everything in the entire universe is made of ever-vibrating energy. Whether it is nonliving or alive, it is all energy. Some energies vibrate slowly and look solid, like for instance your desk or even your Teddy. Some vibrate at a higher speed and may be invisible, like the energy that surrounds all living beings, including us.

"The lower vibrating energies usually stay the same. Like your desk will always be the same - unless it burns up, in which case, it will change its energy to a different form. Our energy, on the contrary, changes every moment. Remember the exercise where I changed my energy just by my thoughts?

"Our energy field's edge is as far as we can reach when we are resting. A healthy aura, which is just a different name for the energy field, forms an egg-shape of energy around our bodies. It would be best if it would stay the same all the time, but it never does. It constantly gets thicker or thinner, clearer or dimmer. These changes happen for various reasons, such as the food we eat, the water we drink, the thoughts we have, the

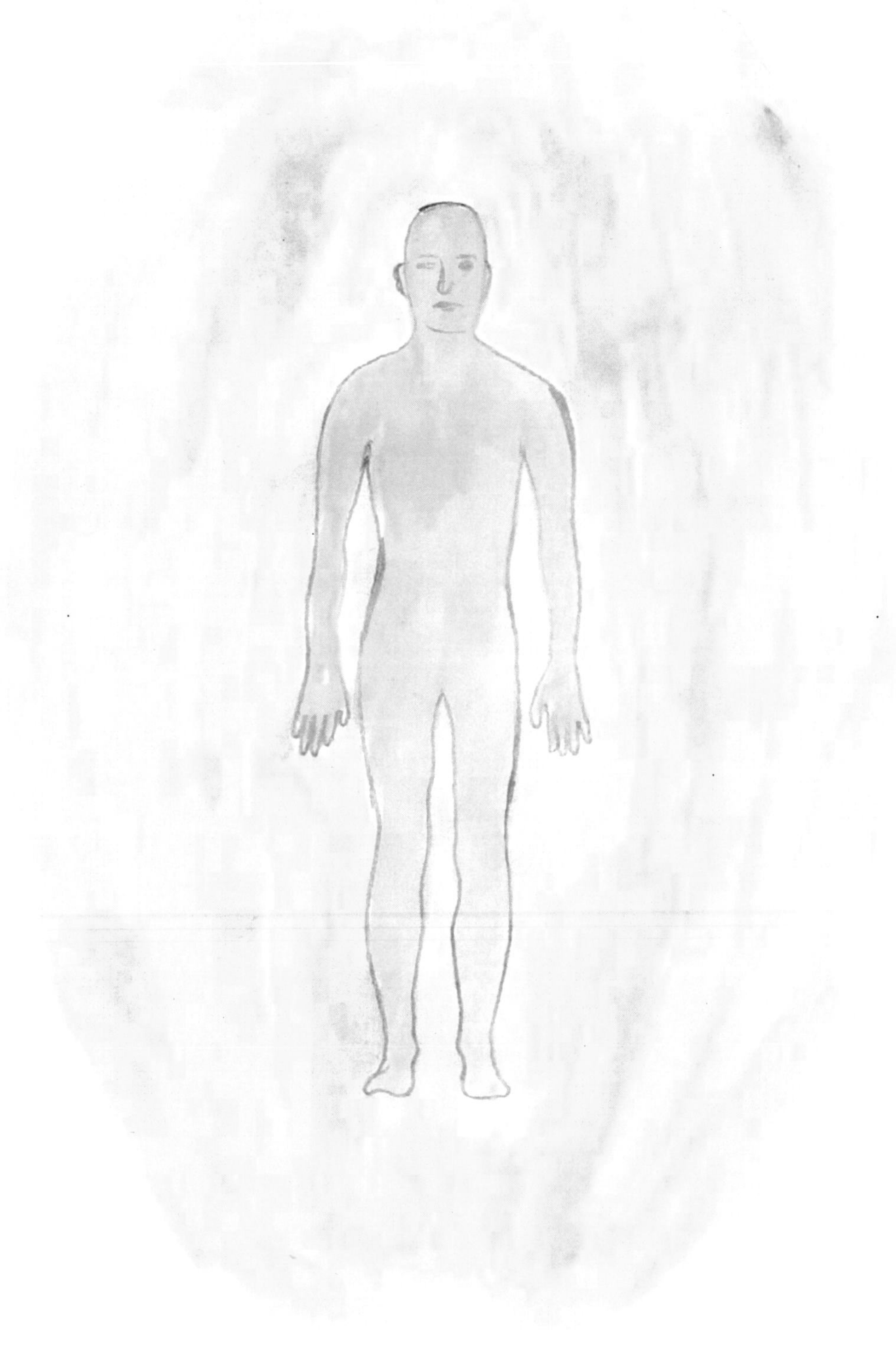

people around us and even our environment. They are all changing our energy all the time.

"Some changes come fast. Some slow. The fastest changes come from our minds. The air we breathe and the foods we eat are also essential. Vibrant, live green foods give us the most energy. That's why I'm so happy when you eat your salad. It is so good for you."

"How about my favorite fruit?" asked Kylie. "Are strawberries good for you?"

"Of course, Kylie," Daddy smiled. "There are many other fruits that are good for you. As a matter of fact, most of them are very healthy. Now let's continue.

"When the change in your aura stays for too long, it results in illness. Some parts of the aura may be too thin for too long, like in case of a cough, where your lungs would have less energy. You can help that by adding energy to the lungs.

"Some parts of the aura may be too thick, as is the case with some headaches. You can stop those by taking the excess energy off. Sometimes, it takes only a few minutes to stop a headache this way."

Kylie listened very carefully. It was way too much information all at once! But she knew she could always ask her Daddy again if she could not remember something. She liked the idea of practicing every day, feeling and seeing the energy. She practiced healing even on her dolls.

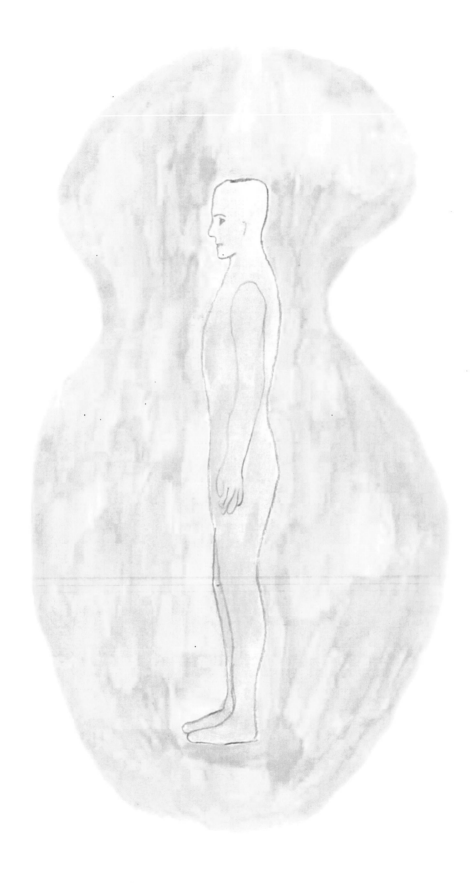

Her Daddy's advice was still ringing in her ears: "If you use your imagination, you will find many other ways to play energy games. You don't have to be able to see your aura all the time to keep it thick and healthy. Especially since the energy games are fun, and fun means positive energy! Keep up with the challenge and the game, and enjoy yourself."

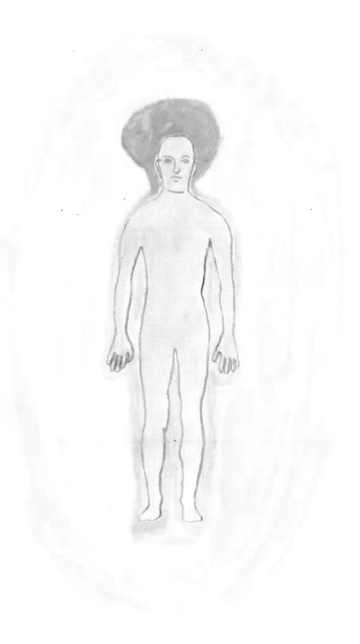

The Little Healer

Kylie took the advice and continued to play the energy games every day. Little did she know that soon these games will be used in a serious way.

A few days later at the daycare, Miss Ana had a terrible headache. It was a really painful headache called a migraine. She was hurting so much that she could hardly keep her eyes open!

Seeing her teacher in so much pain, Kylie decided to help. She had never tried to stop a headache, but she had seen her Daddy do it many times. It is easy: all you have to do is hold the painful areas gently with your hands and then a minute or so later pull the energy off. It sticks to you easily, so you have to shake your hands to get rid of it. You have to repeat it several times. As soon as the extra energy is gone, the headache is gone.

At first Miss Ana didn't like the idea of Kylie touching her achy head, but she gave in anyway. And was she glad she did! As soon as Kylie touched her head she started feeling the heat from her little hands. It was such a pleasant warmth! It spread throughout her whole head, until her head was tingling.

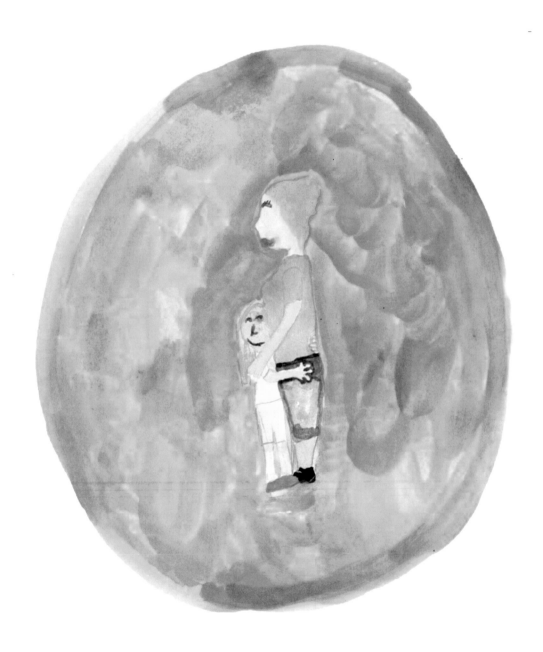

A minute later she was already feeling better. At that time Kylie started pulling the energy away by moving her hands in a sweeping fashion. After every sweep, she would shake her hands to throw away the excess energy. She made sure to cover the entire head with her motions. It worked better than she expected. As the excess energy was coming off, the pain was going away. Within minutes all the pain vanished!

Miss Ana was amazed. She still couldn't understand how this little girl was capable of such an astonishing feat. All the children were amazed, too. Suddenly, everyone wanted to know about Kylie's unbelievable "magic." Nobody ever teased her again. Nobody would dare. She was treated like a hero for the rest of the day. She also got a gigantic hug from her overjoyed teacher.

Kylie could hardly wait to get home to tell her Daddy about her amazing day. She ran into the house, straight to his office, where she almost knocked him over with the force of her excitement. She told him all about her day and what had happened with her teacher. "Daddy, I am a healer now!" she said excitedly.

"I know you are Kylie," Daddy said, "I know you are!" Her Daddy could not have been prouder.

Soon Kylie taught all her friends how to see and how to feel their energy fields, just like Daddy had taught her. She even made up a new game that included standing in a circle and "holding hands" without touching. Amazingly, the kids still felt each other's hands, even though only their auras were touching.

From then on, all the children at the daycare added energy games to their daily play. Some day, they may become great healers, too.

We all have been given special gifts; we all have hidden talents lying within us. Don't be afraid to feel different. That is what makes each one of us the unique individuals who we are.

Feeling, seeing, and using the energy to heal are abilities anyone can master. Even you! Healing is a gift we all have within, just waiting there to be discovered and used for helping others and ourselves.

Now that you have found out about your powers, follow Kylie's lessons, and you too, may become a great healer some day.

PARENTS' GLOSSARY

Aura [**awr**-*uh*]

The electromagnetic field that surrounds the human body and every organism and object in the universe.

In parapsychology, spirituality and New Age belief, an aura is a subtle field of luminous multicolored radiation surrounding a person or object as a cocoon or halo. An aura may reflect the moods, thoughts or state of health of the person it surrounds.

Bioenergy [bahy-oh-en-er-jee]

The subtle energy that permeates and surrounds every living being.

Bio-electromagnetic energy or simply, "living energy" - it is often referred to as Vital Force, Aura, Life Force Energy, Divine Energy, Qi (Ch'i), Ki, Prana, Bioplasma, Animal Magnetism and so on.

Biotherapy [bahy-oh-**ther**-uh-pee]

Short for bioenergy therapy, which is the eastern-European scientific method of energy balancing. It is performed by a practitioner (biotherapist) in order to induce healing.

Energy [en-er-jee]

In this case, the energy of the human being, or bioenergy.

Energy field [en-er-jee feeld]

In this case, the energy in, and around the human body, or bioenergy field.

Healing [**hee**-ling]

The act or process of regaining health – in this case, with the help of a healer.

The natural process by which the body repairs itself.

Healing Energy [**hee**-ling en-er-jee]

In this case, the energy emanating from the healer, or biotherapist.

The energy that helps replenish the body's energy field to induce healing.

Healer [**hee**-ler]

A person or thing that heals.

EPILOGUE

Kylie is ten years old now. She is a bright and active girl, loving animals and arts. She wants to be a marine biologist, an artist, and a healer. She already is the last two.

We practice seeing and feeling the energy quite often, while the healing part comes up when needed.

Kylie's little sister, Karlyn, has also shown interest in the energy healing. Her story is just developing.

Kylie's adventures with her healing powers did not stop at the daycare. That was just the beginning! She continues on her road of learning more about the energy and growing to be a great healer.

Csongor Daniel is an internationally known healer and lecturer. He is the author of <u>Biotherapy: A Healing for the 21st Century</u> as well as numerous articles on health and healing. He also created two exercise videos, the latest being: <u>Energizing T'ai Chi Chi Kung</u>.
Please visit: <u>www.csongordaniel.com</u> for more information.